A Brief Chaos Of Dreams

j.james.g

Dedication

Preface

Acknowledgements

1. Statement of the Shadow

A basic nerve that twists and curves
with all the lessons, but isn't learned.
How does one feel to find a burn,
scorched beneath the skin of Earth?

It's all nonsense that will follow.
That may make dents, but never hollow.
And to think this burn is only borrowed
is to shrink and turn away from sorrow.

Now that nothing has been established
it's time to finish burying the madness;
or make note that nothing may be lavish,
because the ruby tongues are savage.

What was said, was said, was said.
again and again and again.
The reminder to manipulate to mend
is the repetition of the end.

Keep a constant thought awake
to ensure the abundant rot won't take.
Showcasing what is at stake,
creating habits allows optimum space.

2. The [redacted] Address

in an attempt to
be relevant
our eyes were
taken. and
it
wasn't blatant,
but it did
leave
us shaken.
and the fact that
we
cannot
react to the lack
thereof
is proof of lies. it is okay
to
socialize
as long as we
are using
social eyes.it helps to jump
the
line,
but we will dissolve in time.
made to be a filler
when
we
just want to feel more.
designed to be a
thriller,
but there is
too much gore.
it will last as long
as a
cigarette on the set
of the most unheard movie
that
hasn't been made yet.
to all the moons that are brighter than the stars...

the night salutes the fighter showing scars.

3. Letter to the Infinite Findings of Eternity

the trees declined to speak,
while the flowers decided to bloom.
wait for the famous last creaks

when the limbs begin to leak
they will drip across tombs.
there is one that they will greet.

and amidst the saddest meet
a glow will cast the gloom
now they will become streets.

all to brave the concrete -
only visions of doom.
the rings are not discrete.

a mess left to leave,
but is there enough room?
death does never dream.

only at the summit do you find the peak.
how can we keep living; exhume.

a beautiful venation may now bleed.
the Sun's light proving we succeed.

4. A Proclamation of Butterflies

I am engulfed in darkness and looking for light.
I have clawed at the heartless, but I still need more light.

so many caterpillars crawling down my throat.
claiming a spot and getting warmth from the core light.

silver/silver, tongue/stomach - where is the lining?
cardia chrysalis created to store light.

a sickness that is changing and I am grateful.
the feeling of feelings, I want to explore light.

passing teeth out of the cave, it's time to evolve.
the efforts made to flourish, nourish a sore light.

and the fascination of being brave prevails.
the wings will flutter as they take flight and pour light.

the cosmic embrace that takes a lifetime to make,
shall take any name, as long as it adores light.

5. The So-to-mo Admission

I look passed the sky.
I know you are watching me,
'cause I'm still alive.

6. The Beginning Oath

an ambiguous sentiment will not bloom.
i fear it is the definition of a troublemaker.
bad intentions, with distance.
it's rather sad... (and a touch morbid).
a memory of symmetry and thoughts,
are brought forth from decay and rot.
it was as if i was invisible.
the intriguing.
the intense.
the invisible.
it's not the mistake we've made, but it's the mistake we
haven't made.
Time is a gladiator – unnatural, naturally.
take back the rage that created this terror. look in the
mirror.
THIS IS NOT LOVE.
to live: too fun. to die: too young.
a truth teller – you love a burning tongue.
i don't exist happy.
i missed the deadline.
to be incredible, i jumped of the moon.
... as toxic does.

7. The Honey Resolve

the night is dark and the wind calls out,
"who shall save the Honey from the Mouth?"
as it grows darker and darker still,
the taste of death growing near to the kill.
nothing has ever felt so empty of life.
is this to be the end of the night?
can Honey stay sweet with the darkness tightening?
as long as there is something more frightening.

from the oil of alchemy jars -
made of fog with eyes of Pluto and Mars.
a figure forms and storms do cease.
fight abyss with oblivion and see who claims the peace.
Now, growing tall and consuming the depth,
 this villain's-hero will lay to rest –
what once seemed too big to overcome,
now quietly melts and has been overrun.

nothing left but fingernails and teeth.
flowers bloom from the soil of screams.
the darkness has been shown the light,
by the absence of the obvious of night.
as quick as the shadow appeared
it left, only to be feared.

the ones that chase will be sent running,
as sweet to say, it's safe for the Honey.

8. SONNET 727

what a lovely surprise after sunset.
how was life before this moment?
a radiant laugh, although we've not met.
if life was better, it should've shown it.
a curious mind will wander far and wide.
this little expert in creating warmth.
I'll find adventure with you by my side.
you'll move mountains then move forth.
and taking breath that breathes a mess.
you champion connections within the heart.
I'll break all death to give you the rest.
what closes at the end, opens at the start.
to you, my dear, everlasting love will bring.
from you, my dear, ever-feathers on wings.

9. Internal Declaration

in an instant i fashioned precision.
narrowed my focus to experiment.
this is now the reason i am vicious.
i galvanized my teeth so i can eat.
i can't stop once i start to devour.
the passion stokes the phoenix within me.
i'll put the venom (to some) on paper.
this is the poison that draws people in.
the kind that sustained me, read it and weep.
it's the faith behind the words that compel.
it's the smell of the ink that unifies.
things start to grow at the thought of glowing.
the garden of rare youth blossoms at night.
creating the creatures that built the stars.
they were the ones that painted the planets.
they were the ones that drank the milky way.
we are them and they are us, together.
we will now begin to take lust over.
providing that the shades of light stay on.
it is a matter of believing rust.
how happy, are the monsters to trust me.

10. The Da-to-mo Admission

hazel galaxies
searching for what was taken
she knows where to look
but it always takes a toll
Hope knows who you truly are

11. Wisdom Propaganda

the journey stated with a road that was paved (with good intentions).
walking on flat ground, then eventually a slight incline with time.
sometimes there'll be a slight dip and that may wear you down,
but walking on the flat will also wear you down overtime.
so even if you get a slight incline,
you should make the most of it and try and increase the altitude.
I need to take my own advice.

12. A Toast from Underground

mud drips from the fingers of the innocent.
what it meant is more than can be seen.
with a means to know end, it's time to begin.
the lights start to dim, but they're still out walking.
when the chatter turns into talking people start to blink.
it's a little too late to think, but it's time to take action.

there is a limited attraction when being called to action.
but in the latest fashion, we look to the innocent.
searching for the fine print all we do is blink.
blurring the lines and breaking the link just to be seen.
when every street is mean you just gotta keep walking.
in the distance, they are mocking because it's time to
begin.

forming a false grin, the torture may begin.
melting into the chin the plan is taking action.
causing a distraction and the strong hearts are walking.
most are blocking to protect the innocent.
there is a hint of dust, but it won't be seen.
never too clean, but will make you blink.

the drinks are crossed, but don't blink.

when thoughts shrink the dreamer's rebellion must
begin.
to win is to lose, but something that is seen.
again with the dreams, they are the action.
a fraction of the lost are not innocent.
the wild have a glint and are never caught walking

a morose stalking, but thought to be walking.
when the sky starts coughing, the shine makes us blink.
the heart starts to sink searching for the innocent.
even though it's a short stint, it's where the fangs begin.
and now within, we find a heart of action.
and this is passion that has never been seen.

when we believe it's hard not to be seen.
as if the fiend can't stand all the walking.
lips locking in a provocative action.
now light laughter makes the lover blink.
simple on the brink, we must find a way to begin.
the mud sinks in, were they ever really innocent?

this is the action from all that was seen.
the final innocent heart continues walking.
the hard part is to not blink - then we will begin.

13. The Substandard Talk

i heard you fell from the stars.
but I don't know who you are.
your beauty and grace
are too much for this place.
and I am much too bizarre.

14. The Changed Confession

my only wish was not heard.
it must have got taken with the wind.
so now i wait, i know it's absurd.
sorting out what it felt like when I grinned.

yelling at the top of my lungs,
outside of my mind,
undoing when I was young and making up the time.

15. The Darkbird's Call

six men came over the hill in the morning.
with gloom on our face, it gave off a warning.
they walked half a mile, resisting to crawl.
defeated and battered was the look of them all.
by time they got back, they could barely stand.
but they had not lost they had got their man.
for these six men may never fall.

16. Erasure [under]Statement

Biting the
useless
mixture of lies
for the
endless endless.

havoc is
death

C h
a o
s

is exempt

.

17. Scribe Decree

the right and wrong words will come to me.
in the morning, the afternoon, and at night.
these complex thoughts don't make room,
and they will stay out of sight,

the admiration for such intricacies,
is only comparable for a select few.
the power they possess makes me swoon.
they will leave you breathless, too.

so vast with feelings of every single kind.
it is hard enough no to choke on them.
the swelling in my chest and head,
once a seedling, I'm only still a stem.

18. The Framework Claim

a heart beats days away (w e e k s . . . m o n t h s. . . . y e a r s . . . really).
and I can't find the time to make myself known?
give me a break[down].
as if I need my cover blown or maybe I made shoes of stone.
either way, when I escape I'll have to coerce fate.
I'll grab the stars and align them myself.
and these scars are not made by anybody else.
let me take this time to create a breath.
cross the line and coerce death.
I could ramble on for days (w e e k s . . . m o n t h s. . . . y e a r s . . . really).

19. The Here Agreement

the ghosts wait on the edge of the woods,
and I walk amongst the gravestones.
there jonathan laid where I now stood,
while he sleeps he is not alone.

20. Closing Perceptions

it was nice to know you.
because you are nice.
only as long as it is true.

it was great, but at what price?
and things change so quickly.
are there others that entice?

"how could someone pick me?",
dissolve within the tears.
it's me who knows love, strictly.

the rainy days are starting to clear.
I'm not mad or angry, I'm just...
it will be hard to not have you near.

I rise up from the rust,
incomplete but made of lust.

21. The Invisible Doctrine

can you hear the wind crying?
I hear it every night.
are you even trying?
it is keeping out of sight.

I hear it every night.
it begs for love and mercy.
it is keeping out of sight.
it has seen the worst me.

it begs for love an mercy.
I tell it to be patient.
it has seen the worst me.
I'll forever chase it.

I tell it to be patient.
can you hear the wind crying?
I'll forever chase it.
are you even trying?

www.ingramcontent.com/pod-product-compliance
Lightning Source LLC
Chambersburg PA
CBHW070725160726
48003CB00006BA/2387